The Window

THE WINDOW

POEMS BY *Vern Rutsala*

Wesleyan University Press
MIDDLETOWN, CONNECTICUT

Library of Congress Catalog Card Number: 64–22374

Manufactured in the United States of America

FIRST EDITION

TO JOAN

Contents

The Window

PART I

Gardening

Waking, afraid to touch
    the wound that morning
    has inflicted, we turn and
    lift the bandage of the blinds.
    Beyond the window
    wind-up birds totter
    seeming to listen to the grass.

In our yard the weeds
    are doing well and give
    their seeds to any wind
    that blows, even to our
    wordless neighbors who try,
    it seems, to set the world
    straight each day with hoes
    and hoses. Their hands
    are all green thumbs that
    test the pulse of twigs.

Sitting back, we watch their
    rituals of the spring.
    In clothing carefully aged
    they work and work
    prying flowers from their dirt
    or pinching bushes until
    the welts of buds appear.

Pausing, they scout
    with glances the No Man's Land
    of our yard which must

for them conceal mines;
or they long, perhaps,
to harness the worms
that wander our bloomless soil.

In the bands of shade
taped below the brims
of their straw hats,
their pious eyes float,
possibly irrigated by tears
for all our wild grass
that aches for the quick
teeth of a mower.
But they are busy people
and so they bend again
to tease color from their dirt.

Over what breakfast we find,
we watch them poke for frail
tendrils under stones
and imagine that they
dream all day of times
when they will pose,
sunburned and earthy,
beside their prize azaleas.
But our flowering weeds
bother them and we half-expect
to see them at night
quietly pawing our yard,
burying dead seeds
they hope the moonlight
will make green again
or cutting out the hearts
of our undisciplined weeds.

Below their calloused knees
    well-known and indifferent
    worms labor and digest
    lost in thoughts of length
    and the coiling of links
    designed to invade
    the very cells of secrets.
As roots explore earth,
    grubs assemble and receive
    assignments. And while the neighbors
    work hunting worms and flowers,
    flowers and worms
    wait patiently for them.

Late

1.

Up late, ripping next day's calendar
with a drink, he pounds her
shopping bag with curses across
the room. He sees danger in its design,
a sack to contain his life:
his life, a weight he must carry
seven damned days a week.
He crushes the hands of the clock
with a business grip. This done,
he arranges the parts on the carpet
and dances. He must find, he knows,
an agony of his own choice.
Cookbooks were not written
to please him. Darker covers
conceal the phrases of his needs.

2.

Conscripted by sleep, she feels the calendar
tear listlessly, making a scar on her
midnight. Darkness is only a ride across
the desert of days. Without design,
tomorrow she will walk on life
thinking herself a pivot to carry
the damp weight of each week.
On the bedside table she hears the clock
disrobe and give up time to what is done
each night on her sunbleached carpet.
In sleep, prowling her dreams, she knows
his approach. Nightly, he brings her choice
of him to bed; on her body are written
the angry bruises, locked beneath covers,
of the furtive destitution of his needs.

Fears

The streets are dark. Stray dogs—
old blankets thrown over sticks—
examine the life of alleys
while simple enemies in pool halls
practice their assaults with cues,
long and wooden. Grinning, they nod
at each woman on each corner.

But somewhere, in a dusty room perhaps—
where he hides from a loving wife—
the man waits amusing himself by plotting
all the routes of women who come home late.
By climbing lamp posts and unscrewing bulbs
he prepares the streets and then crouches
in shadow stroking his mustache and listening
for the delicate step of embroidered maidens who bring
the feather boa of their innocence to his hands.

The ladies, pursed lips daring
the dark to leap at them, stroll sedately
and behind rimless glasses their eyes prod alleys
as they plan the stories they will tell
and the weeks devoted to recovery.
Each night they wander all the streets,
poking at the shadows with their eyes,
imagining the unwashed man who must hide there
aching for the dry biscuits of their bodies.

The Institution

Someone, working steadily at night
by dropping water from his canteen,
has worn grooves in the steps
leading to columns pitted as chewed pencils.

The windows are like deep-set eyes;
the door is a leather-bound book no one has read.
A commemorative plaque is worn smooth
as an old coin by many kisses—

just as, inside, the leaders have lost their toes
from wading in the blind reverence
of the people. Terra-cotta statues of them
line the entrance hall; they each have slots

in the top like children's banks.
A former hero dozes on a folding chair
chasing the wounded cats of his sleep.
Feet on marble sound like spoons tapping eggs.

Large, furtive insects like pageboys
stare from the shadows and run along
the baseboards. Outside the meeting chamber
a justice of the peace bandages his eyes.

Inside the chamber a school of vagrants
studies leisure or rolls endless cigarettes.
A special subcommittee is in session
planning obscure illnesses for us.

Marriage Contract

No one spells out the unwritten agreement,
the fine unphrased concessions made
between the two parties.

She, party of the first part,
protects him from seeing his own face
on mirrored walls. She covers the glass
with delicate pictures, subtle drawings
which equal his imagined self as he
lumbers through halls breaking china,
shattering delicate glass and smiling
a ludicrous grin at dreams of himself.

He, party of the second part, accepts
his role and plays the crude but sensitive man.
In the night he practices his gait,
lumbering through dreams of flowers,
breaking the stems of trees, hiding
his own soft face like mollusc flesh
within the grinning shell
he's sworn by secret law to wear.

Thorpe, Nurmi, Ruth

Smooth muscles tic. Honeyed sunlight
spreads thickly on stadium grass.
Drinkers of grace shout throats dry,
voices hoarse for the quiet moment.

He, below on the stippled grass,
circles back slipping smooth leather
on his palms, dancing on the cinders.
Racing scything Time, he smiles.

The ball, an empty eggshell, spirals
over long shadows in left field
searching for the wall. He turns
watching its fragile flight, gauging

its fall as if he, a fireman, were
coaxing some hysteric from burning sills.
The moment goes. He jogs up field,
eases to the bench, rides shoulders to showers.

Bijou

Huge, perfect creatures move across the screen
to the rhythms of hidden bands.
Small, imperfect creatures slouch in plush seats
and pull crystal tears from their eyes
when the intellectual dog is lost
or when the nearly nice supporting player
is culled from the action by a villain arrow
while saving the blond-souled hero.
They drop their tears and look around hopefully
when they hear the bugle of a rescue party.
But the aisles are empty. Odorless horses
sprint onto the screen below waving flags.

The Town Square

They are still there moving in the doom
of sunlight. Near the City Hall, in the shade,
old men are playing euchre. Light
glints from the metal parts
of their suspenders, rubbed white by use.
And near them their substitutes
wait for a time-out to enter the game.
Nothing new. Each Saturday the same.

But if you listen: "Each day contains
the bud of small ferocities. We wait,
our eyes dimming like old light bulbs—
within, the faint sound of broken filaments—
and long to begin again. We lounge, we read
the national news: 'And she wrote a year before:
Perhaps I've begun to find my way . . .
The autopsy of vital organs revealed nothing.'

"And the kites of our desire snap
in a blue wind. They blossom before
power lines scythe their veins, stiff
as armatures. At home our taps
drip acid. The taverns of our souls
are empty, each cup empty.
We wait our turn at euchre."

Lovers in Summer

Near the frayed edges of towns,
    the places where roads tire
    of their coats of tar
    and shed them to run bare
    in the dust; there, paired
    lovers roll in the grass
    wrapped in halos of insects,
    wreathed by summers of loneliness.

Out in the country others pretend
    to romp in haylofts,
    mimicking the motions
    of animals, making
    themselves seem robust
    though their bones
    bear the long-planted
    seeds of rickets. Their limbs
    are bowed and thin,
    full of future fractures
    and undiscovered limps.

Elsewhere initials are carved
    in the soft bark
    of sentiment and eternal
    pledges are made.
    Nights are ripe
    with affirmations
    heard through echo chambers.
    And young men scratch
    their knees on the pebbles
    of their proposals.

Muted, perspiring, the long
nights of adolescence
continue in obscure
parking places where
engagements have been
sealed and bruises found
among cool leatherette.
The marathons of their lives
have come to this:
they hear the parched
runners of their blood
approaching to light
victory fires
in their groins.

And everywhere in rooms
the lamps go down,
the record players play
and parents strain
near sleep to hear
the sounds of zippers,
the tentative noises
of bedrooms, the voices
of couch springs
that accompany
each sugary moan.

Playground

From a bench I watch
the grass spread out,
climbing a knoll,
falling into a pool,

looking for the enameled
sheep that are its due.
This lawn is forced
to be green

by the attendant
who coils and uncoils
the drugged snakes
of the hoses, letting them

feed all day
at deep mains.
On the playground
patient children

are learning how
to break the rules
day by day. I see
the cheat, quick hands

making ready
for a future of short
change; the liar
practices his surgery

on the real; and the fool
wears his freckles
like a mask, buckteeth
grinning at the beautiful.

And the outlines appear
here, too, of those
who will always
obey the rules: the informer,

the self-righteous,
leaning into their
peculiar blindness.
Scattered over the field

the graceful and the sure,
those few married
to certainty, score
winning runs and aim

toward disease.
The lovers and the doomed
grow tan, and the good
are somehow learning
the punishing arts
of their losing game.

Sunday

Up early while everyone sleeps,
I wander through the house,
pondering the eloquence
of vacant furniture, listening
to birdsong peeling
the cover off the day.

I think everyone I know
is sleeping now. Sidewalks
are cool, waiting for
roller skates and wagons.
Skate keys are covered
with dew; bicycles look
broken, abandoned on the lawns—
no balance left in them,
awkward as wounded
animals. I am the last
man and this is my
last day; I can't think
of anything to do. Somewhere
over my shoulder a jet
explores a crease
in the cloudy sky;
I sit on the porch
waiting for things to happen.

O fat god of Sunday
and chocolate bars, watcher
over picnics and visits to the zoo,
will anyone wake up today?

Near Rivers, Under Bridges

Admired from picture windows
or the scenic viewpoint,
the American sun goes down
like a perfect reproduction.

Arbiters of sunsets sigh or trot
into their enameled kitchens
certain once again that what is
is good, wishing only for a rainbow.

But near rivers, under a new
overpass launched like a narrow sky
of concrete thickly clouded,
a deeper night invites its patrons.

Insured and dedicated to safety
but for the King's X of holidays,
wheels thunder overhead shaking
fragments down on the sailor on leave

who steers dimes toward a juke box
over eggshells of the night before.
Farther off, gathering sidewalks in the bristles
of his broom, a janitor pushes

to high stools as rain pocks his denims
and he anticipates another supper
of pepperoni from jars, fish swimming
dryly in cellophane or popcorn heated by a bulb.

Plump sightseers have followed lights
of dashboards to their homes; night
has brushed black over all picture windows.
But some walk dimly followed by bands

beating salvation or waiting in ambush
around some corner with tambourines
muffled in rags, faces blackened, music
zeroed in on the sentiments of sidewalks.

And the sun has gone down for others
where neon streaks methodically their torn
manila blinds, old maps on the darkness
of their windows, or glitters dully

on iron bedsteads. Later they walk
all night, sometimes frightening cats in alleys,
sometimes leaning in the coffin of a doorway,
uncertain of what is, waiting for a sunrise.

The Incomplete

Bad weather seems to turn them up
as you move, stooped by the burden
of roofs, in attics or above garages
and sift the anonymous clutter to find
those things that fingers dropped
like half-smoked cigarettes:
The model plane dry as a mounted insect,
its rubber motor only a pencil line
along the stunted fuselage; sweaters dank
as feed sacks, each with only one sleeve
that waits for some distant uncle
to lose an arm to moths; vacations
shut tight in rolls of undeveloped film;
or half-read books that float
face down near the debris of a lawn chair.

Such dwarfs persist, seeming to prosper
in the dust. Lives begun with each advantage
but lost like coins through gratings.
Slipped from thought like that relative
whose heart winced and then failed after ping pong,
whose grave is now overgrown and cluttered
as the drawers of ancient bureaus.
Or more, perhaps, like those blond children
who, after wading, felt skin tighten and seem
to shrink and so took their puckered fingers
to garages where they oiled the hinges
of old ice boxes and then grew very cool and quiet.

Nightfall

Night settles like a damp cloth
over the houses. The houses that are shut,
that show no wear. Lawns
are patrolled by plywood flamingoes
or shrubbery clipped from magazines.

Nightlocks have been put to work,
their single fists tight in the wood.
Within, each floor has been swept
until bone shines through. Each light bulb
has been washed and polished.

And now the readers of newspapers,
those who savor the taste of box scores,
recline in chairs that have perfect postures.
Air ruffles dry ferns on mantels
and touches intricate clocks beneath bell jars.

A pipe is tamped with a lacquered hand.
Repose flutters in match flare and a face
is turned toward a window. Then, as if seeing
eyes pressed like stamps to the glass,
it turns quickly and lunches on want ads.

Others recline, the army of competence,
the many firm turners of lathes,
the knowledgeable numbers who know
the secrets of fuse boxes, the tricks
of storm windows, the precision with which

flagstones must indent the grass.
They lean back, these artists of roasts,
these heads of tables, listening

to dishes shift in warm water,
hearing bills collect on their doorsteps

like gypsies. Night drops firmly.
Now the second car sleeps beside the first.
The committee meetings are over
and each chairwoman prepares late snacks
of corsages and pewter door prizes.

Some turners of lathes move
toward dreams where they wear
masks with great cleft chins.
Some wives watch their phones grin
at their unused appointment pads.

Others think of daughters driven
to seek, late at night, hot solace
on leather couches; or of sons, failures
as halfbacks, forced to mold cars
around power poles. But they move

toward sleep letting dreams float
as in the tips of fingers. But some
lie awake, chairwomen and handymen,
with thought welded to a single
nipple of light, the glow of a cigarette.

For them the next day treads heavily
in each tick of the clock and they lie
with thoughts moving from the frail glow
inward into a mesh of wires, a fusion
of days and dates, bank accounts

or formal dances years before.
Memories shift scraping along

the tender mind. They remember
those cuts that will not heal,
those growths they cannot explain,

those slights that at the time
seemed meaningless and now grow cancerous.
Some stare steadily into blackness
afraid that they are blind, testing
their blindness. Some listen

to the burglar sounds of their sleeping
houses. Dawn lies coiled in clocks.
There are no conclusions. The dark is there.
Cigarettes burn down and are ground out
in souvenir ashtrays from vacations by the sea.

PART II

Looking in the Album

Here the formal times are surrendered
to the camera's indifferent gaze: weddings,
graduations, births and official portraits taken
every ten years to falsify appearances.
Even snapshots meant to gather afternoons
with casual ease are rigid. Smiles
are too buoyant. Tinny laughter echoes
from the staged scene on an artificial
beach. And yet we want to believe
this is how it was: That children's hair
always bore the recent marks of combs;
that trousers, even at picnics, were always
creased and we traveled years with the light
but earnest intimacy of linked hands or arms
arranged over shoulders. This is the record
of our desired life: Pleasant, leisurely on vacations,
wryly comic before local landmarks, competent
auditors of commencement speakers, showing
in our poses that we believed what we were told.
But this history contains no evidence
of aimless nights when the wilderness of ourselves
sprang up to swallow the outposts of what
we thought we were. Nowhere can we see
tears provoked by anything but joy. There
are no pictures of our brittle, lost intentions.
We burned the negatives that we felt did not give a true
account and with others made this abridgement of our lives.

Midnight

For Joan

Twelve sprawls on the night
with sharp noises and long silence.
Lights have clicked off
in imitation of all neighbors.
Dust ghosts slide under doors
and settle on shiny tables to accuse
dull housewives on dull mornings.

Stars stretch beyond windows
in the yawning sky. (Midnight is distance
and the sounds of sleeping fathers
that hum through the trees
and over houses.) Our watches tell the hour
that stays all night around limp children
drowned in sleep. Then silence
is chipped by a confused rooster
that crows at the quick daylight
of a passing car, and then forgets this day
like all those that have forgotten
his spurs and bright feathers.

The stars switch on and off
like eyes startled by the sight of earth.
(Our beds revolve slowly
around the moon and prowl the flat night
looking for morning.)

The Funeral

Scarcely touching silence
the usher whispered
as he passed among us
dispensing sympathy
even though his feet
were lost, contributed
by his ankles
to the carpet's depth.

But we shuffled
as if on skis
across that waste of rug,
unsure of where death
lay, in which corner
he would be propped,
smiling as he
shopped among us.

The rooms wore mutes;
hushed insects moved
on padded feet;
curtains, like towels,
absorbed each sound
that overflowed the rug.

And we thought
the silence must be
for someone asleep—
exhausted after a long
trip, fitfully near
the edge of waking.

The walls
grew tongues and music
sprouted, too near,
and in light bleeding
through stained glass
we saw an effigy
of the person
who had died for us
by telegram.

Visits

Strangers invade
the dim facades.
The cracked leather
flanks of suitcases
mutter like saddles.
Cousins test each other
on chinning bars
before their heights
are measured back to back.
And soon the houses change:
Daybeds convert
themselves obsequiously
to night duties.
Rooms are disarrayed:
Like weak triangles
metal coat hangers
on doorknobs
ring the dim tunes
of all reunions.

Asylum

Expecting eyes to mar the windows—
expecting fences, barbed wire, perhaps guards in towers,
the visitors approach slowly.
The place seems almost natural—
like the campus of a Baptist school:
neat, green and sanitary.

Once inside, the visitors sit as if aware
of an accident that is to occur
while their backs are turned. Perhaps a drunken bus
will smash the plaster hours of the afternoon,
perhaps their cigarettes will explode. They do not know
and so seem content to sit
and drum their fingers absently.

But the accident has already occurred
and the visitors are stupid when they are shown
results not reported in the papers,
not noticed on the icy streets.
And within muscled walls ignorant of weather
they watch storms bleed in someone's eyes.

Listening

Outside tonight, earth stretches
    tight as canvas over buds of birth
    that nibble, unseen, at a silence
    stitched loosely with insect sounds.

Along the hall doors crouch to conceal
    noises that press blades to their backs.
    We listen while a dustpan eats
    the scattered pieces of a quarrel.

And elsewhere the bees of love are angry
    as voices predict the distant silence
    of divorce with words that apologies
    will dilute but never cleanse.

Domesticity rumbles in the walls
    as waterpipes and drains indicate
    that number six has bathed and now seeks
    one-armed love, lost beneath his blankets.

Next door, locked behind a fear of sudden
    thunder, a child draws stick figures
    of his absent parents and then
    with cries tears them to confetti.

Farther down the hall coughs reveal
    the aging couple, dry as gourds, for whom
    the spring night has bred a yellow
    sickness that chokes the grass

And makes crickets clatter like rusty saws.
>
> For them the tinder of birth has smoldered
> and gone out. They only await the blinding
> scrap of sight before the whole dun world fades.

Avidly, we hear this news of other life
> with ears pressed into the flowered paper
> of our walls. Camouflaged, itching among petals,
> we pray they will remain unnoticed

As we listen for hints of ways
> to live; but we find that other rooms
> contain no answers—only lives
> as littered and remorseful as our own.

Onset

The trees, branches naked
as whips, house no birds;
grass has stopped growing,
stunted by cold, waiting
for brittle sleep under snow;
the house shudders, discovering
all the warped boards
bought by summer. A broken
shutter comes to life
in this wind. We hear
its sound, sensing the cry
in the single rusted hinge.
We know that 'weathered'
has a meaning now
it fails to have, spread
with August's heavy light.
Blue boards acquire color
by living through such winters;
and even summer gives
the silent gift of worms,
their gouged places filled tonight
by the whistling storm.
Now is the time that things
fall down: apples become boulders
too heavy for the trees
and fall to find bruises
among the tinder of the leaves.

The Improvement

These are the addicts of charts,
the anxious who wait for crises
and side effects, their eyes geared
to read only the scrawls of doctors.
They sit in their lawn chairs
at late evening, hoping the voices
from the high grass will stop,
that they will someday hold
a mower in their hands again
and never sit undressed while doctors
thump their chests like melons.
Something will happen, they know.
The latest abscess applying for admission
to their flesh will prove a fraud;
their x-rays will turn out to be
those of someone else; and they
will be made to lose their appetite
for the fumes of motors in locked garages.
But the voices go on, calling them
to join the dark burrowers, the faint
turners of soil, on distant vacant lots
where only the dismembered
or decaying are discovered.
But they always save their shining
trump for late evening's final
desolation: They say all weakness
finds its compensation—the blind
hear the steps of ants, the deaf read
whispers and the incurable never die.

Illness at Home

1. A musty quiet enters the house
as if it were infected too,
with blinds grown too limp
to rise and let in the sun
and rooms careless about their appearance:
salves and pills gather on all
endtables and couches wear
wrinkled blankets. You can
almost hear the paint begin
to peel from the walls as if
a blight had struck the wood
and doors only waited to be labeled
quarantined or condemned.

2. No one wears shoes. There is
the hush of slippers
and the cold keen sound
of pans being rinsed—the sharp
whine as the final spurt
drives from the faucet and the last
ringing swirl and echo
when the pan is bumped.
The healthy move silently
and do much sitting in the kitchen
reading the messages
in coffee cups. Their talk
is muted as consultations.

3. Everyone moves slowly,
weighed down with the burden
of the sick body they attend—
weak with the weight
of those shadowed eyes on their
backs. All become nurses—
but not those metallic statues
in the corridors of hospitals—
rather they are like the orderlies
on battlefields, driven
to numbness by the helpless pity
the dressing stations
demand from them.

Weak Heart

A chill loosens his
thought. Seasons are changing
shale-deep in the earth.
He hears the strata

gnashing, the grinding
of sea-bottom ranges.
The clams are at war
in the sand. Lichens

will capitulate. All
consent to be coral.
Somewhere in his chest
a beat goes thin;

he feels the soft blur—
the caged moth fighting
with wings for weapons,
crisper than leaves. World,

he says, I walk
the alleys of fear.
Caution, my beacon,
dwindles to nothing.

My hand is a stranger;
my heart is an enemy
I cannot allow
to surrender.

Loosed by the quiet of a house
where each squandered implement
finally rests—each knob points
toward "off" and the evening
congeals in the silent, oiled
interiors of unwound clocks—
my thoughts struggle
in the worn light toward some meaning
the quiet churns in the dark.
Figures of the day just lived
form and dissolve on the window
where rain washes with a wild hand.
Deep in the cells of nerves
the recent past revives and I see again
how the usual aimless beads
of action were strung on the knotted
twine of time, shaping the gristle
of the day that we can chew
but never swallow. All acts
that swirled from the depths
of malice now dance in the dark, mounted
in the past like paste jewels
to be worn to the grave.
But what can be done now?
Should we scatter handbills of apology
to the world? We know
we cannot simply charm
our goodness out, that it lies
hidden in marine depths
far below the surfaces of days,
that any supply of it is greater
than the demand. We know, too,

that here in the soothing night
we are victims of our own
polite excuses for ourselves;
yet we still long for a morning
when we will finally snap
our chrysalis and become a flying thing,
vying for perfection, a hero
for the eye, a gracious winner.
Around each of us, houses breathe.
Electricity gathers in wires
and phones crouch, preparing
to deliver poisonous messages.
We muffle our thoughts
under the warmth of blankets
afraid to enter
the panic country of our dreams
without the badge of sleep.

The Books

Locked in place on their shelves,
haphazard—Insight near Information,
Pleasure beside Conduct—
the books talk of the past
as all things do, spelling out
old enthusiasms, dusty
and yellowing. Margins are clear,
still waiting for our long arguments,
civilized and passionate,
with dead authors. Now the jackets
fade, read by the sun, looking
for the torn places of use,
each asking to be the favorite
carried on all our journeys
or worn like a medal to stop bullets
aimed from the ambush
of drowsy adventures. Browsing,
we ask: When was that read?
What did it say? A thin tune
rises in the mind and dwindles
down an alley tangled with wires
and rubbish, ending at a brick
wall, the dead end of sense
and memory. We wander there,
minor figures in a forgotten
novel, lost in an early chapter.

Five O'Clock Meditation

The hour's sound is signaled repeatedly
    as if factories and mills were ships
    impatient to get through locks to sleep.
    All day, near the town, they rolled
    sprinkling ashes over linens
    that stiffen on lines in winter,
    ghosts salted and hung to dry.

And now the crippled residue of daylight
    stumbles through a park,
    leans here and there on a tree,
    blazing an aimless trail, or lies
    torn as fruit rind on grass
    pushed like needles through the dirt.

The whistles opened lids of darkness
    and along democratic roads workers
    of all kinds sift toward their homes,
    lunch pails now carrying sandwiches
    of waxpaper, ghosts of energy daubed
    in the white of their knuckles on steering
    wheels. The day is deflated. Minutes are now
    flat as run-over carcasses as cars
    turn up graveled drives, beetles
    haunting the quieter streets.

And seen through the foliage of years
    old friends, former sharers of secrets,
    seem to skate along the walks,
    their forms winking between the trees,
    caught in acts the future has forbidden.
    Approaching night plants them

on remembered corners before calls
pluck them to wither once again
around supper tables, to be battered
by the heavy serving spoons and bruised
beneath their parents' stone affections.

What seeds of illness were sown
    in that past now flickering between trees?
    What innocence, lacquered by habit,
    grew stiff as knives to carve
    the first erosive marks of middle age?
    What made them arrive at their own tables
    where they sit gorging themselves
    on the thin energies of their own children,
    frail as willows? Some morning
    youth left willing them their bodies
    and their appetites and turned
    the blades of their anger to dull
    grudges they now carry all day
    like wounds they refuse to treat.

They have left the street; night
    has dissolved all alleys to the past.
    They sit in rooms with those
    their younger selves promised love—
    a love now scissored to the size
    of childish but coronary valentines.

PART III

Before a Journey

The day ends and the entire state
lumbers toward its barns,
praying once more that hay
will remain asbestos

for another night. Doors
are locked on that huge,
toothed machinery of execution
now slumbering in greasy shade,

dreaming of the limbs
it will eat at harvest.
All across the fields
murmured grace is the whirring

of locusts over landscapes
of dumplings; denim ghosts
haunt our waking—
an army locked in garrison.

At such times our lives
are worn out, combustible
as rags that once were
finery, and we feel

shored up in tombs,
surrounded by possessions
without use. Rough fingers
paw our thoughts,

unearthing exhortations:
"Get out you damned fool;
leave this world of churns
and sheds. Follow blistered

highways to a green place.
Here, stapled in the present,
you are only someone's
random thought,

given breath by accident,
only having roles
in the whispered closet dramas
of another's gossip."

The New House

This place is not ours:
the window sill refuses
to wear our drying wishbone
and the floors don't fit

the worn spot for carpets
we seem to take
everywhere we go.
The house still sings

its own tune, sending
our footsteps along the floor
through timbers that creak
to keep the basement washer

company, peopling that lair
of webs and laundry
where the furnace lifts
its arms to warm

the rooms. But the rooms
are cold, bent
on remembering
other hands caressing

woodwork with soft cloths
and feet that always
tiptoed. Wallpaper
has memorized

the places where
their pictures hung.
Soon enough, we know,
the rooms will give in.

Our own mice will shatter
cupboards and later
we will sprain our wrists
opening new bills.

But last night
windows threatened
to bring in the storm
and the back door banged

and banged, giving us
a message we could understand,
something menacing and wooden
that spoke, asking us to travel

to the storm's blind, silent eye.

The Poet at Twenty-Seven

The mind, that slow sea creature,
has again begun its drifting
and I think of the long hallways
wit must follow to find a way
to light: Through deep corridors
of coral, passing waving sea grass
and the eyeless, armored fish.

But today I have lost my place
in all the helpful handbooks.
Thoughts simply float among wrecks
discarded by the surface, and I feel
that art demands better weather,
steadier hands than I discover
strapped to my wrists today.

The happy poets always find
some thing—pressed flowers,
a plaster bust—that is water-
tight and holds the powders
of their sense; but in this room
all objects are sieves
wearing the fingerprints

and bent corners of use.
None will hold the meanings
of lives run aground at night—
of hulls foundered in stairwells
containing soaked and spoiled cargo.
I think of the bald eloquence
events all have that words must steal.

I walk around the room,
stop at the frosted windows
and draw on them: a bleeding
valentine, a hanged man—
works of art for such a winter—
and long for coves where thought
may swim but is never forced to dive.

The Cough

Lately it's awakened me
at night—
a noose pulled tight
or a hand, taloned and warty,
around my throat.

A cough, like the hook
of a winch in my chest,
reeling me
into the grit-strewn light
of three A.M.

I feel that something
is loosening—knitting
is unraveling,
glue is letting go,
boards are shedding their nails.

Something is trying
to wrench me awake,
someone is trying to speak.
A person—voiceless, alone—
kept hidden within me.

Intermission

Offended, we turn away.
This was not it, not intended:

The hero is old, a fat man
greasy with many meals,

his voice nervous, prone
to clot with emotion

and crack at the expected
moment. This was not it.

We wanted a better king;
in fact, a man fit for horses

spitting mercy and curses
on everyone, us as well.

But we found only this pompous
doorman wearing a rancid

uniform, tripping over swords
and too conscious of his epaulettes.

A Day in March

For Joan and Matthew

I awoke that day to the usual
weakness of morning: my senses
random as broken beads.
        The day before

Spring had been near:
buds inched along paralytic twigs,
near waking, numb rumors
        that promised birth.

But that morning the buds
were gone, muffled by sudden snow
spilled over them by midnight.
        Yet birth was going on,

we knew, straining steadily
beneath those white sheets
and today we would count
        the intervals

between each spasm.
And it seemed to us
that to mark the day the world
        had slowed,

shuddered to a halt and brought
out its regal beasts, the lumbering
and lowing snowplows, to parade
        in honor of the event.

For several were trying to be born
that day: a child and a mother

and a father who would find
    their names the moment

new lungs protested the bite
of air. Snow remained,
resisting the blandishments
    of the sun;

day and night passed
and while each of you wrestled
with the problem of being born
    I sat rubbing out

cold thoughts read into my brain
by tales of broken births.
Outside, streets were clearing.
    Salt and sand

had chewed the snow to grit
and the long winter ended
when spring rode in
    on a cry.

Apportioning a Day of Leisure: Time Chart

1.
Wheeled efficiency roams the street
and here, behind doors
like shut safes, we try to mimic it,
hoarding the currency of ourselves
and of the time that stumbles in our veins.

What should be done? Donate
a sentimental hour to the yard
watching squirrels imitate our desires
by making silos of the trees?
Or perhaps we should rearrange our books

placing them once again according to
size and publisher. Then, there is always
argument to ignite morsels of our time
until exhaustion orders us to bed.
(Perhaps two hours for argument.)

Meditation, too, is legitimate. We try
it in darkened rooms until the past,
approaching on moccasins of guilt,
attacks with bits of our broken words.
They spot the darkness. (Ten minutes.)

2.
The day is a meal that must be
consumed. In the morning we can read
papers for an hour and learn of lives
where collars never fray and silver
never tarnishes; or of some neighbor

become the victim of a gas main,
blown far beyond his church. But afternoon
yawns ahead. Should we walk measuring
the weather? Should we lie in wait
for evenings flickering with movies?

Oh hell, the hours spill about us
waiting to be filled. Their only shape
is on our watches where they lie nailed.
But they open and we enter
wondering how much time should be

devoted to our time charts.
But the day is like a system of halls
angled with mirrors where our acts
echo with the indecision of limping steps
or like hours lie nailed to the clocks.

February 5

Slipped in scabbards of ice, trees lean
toward a future of firewood. Birds
are clipped to their twigs like ornaments,
song must be chipped from frozen throats.
Drunks are sleeping blindly under drifts
in parking lots. North is all around us.
Our very names are numb, static
in the rooms, afraid to go beyond our doors
with us. So, anonymous, we move
through unknown streets, dumb, delivering
each step as we search cotton swabbing
sidewalks for footprints left there
years before. And like a moth seeking warmth
age huddles behind us near porchlights
waiting patiently to find the wounds
we leave in the snow—the trail we will
follow when age joins us years from now.

The Fat Man

I call everyone
shriveled. Dried apples
fit for cellars,
nothing more.
They have no folds,
no flesh to touch—
gangling reminders
of the grave.

Existence melts
in my mouth.
I relish, I taste
the sweet jams of life;
I gorge and worship
the place of love:
all kitchens everywhere.

Diet is sin:
an effort
to turn limbs
to razors that slice
a lover's hands.
Right angles
pierce my eye;
I love the arc,
soft ovals, the curve—
things molded
to be touched,
the soothers of sight.

I feel at least
ten souls
swimming in my flesh.
I feed them
with both hands.
Someday
I will become
a mountain.
I eat the world.

Statement from an Apartment

The pictures on our walls
are never seen.
No one marks shifts
in the tones of our voices

or sees our small gestures
of remorse and loss
in exclamations over
the episode of the broken

dish. No one hears the elegies
of our footsteps move to where
we formally mourn the death
of days with toothbrush

and mouthwash.
No guerrillas hide
in the hills of our paintings,
lethal silence falling

from their garrotes.
We have placed blindfolds
on all the keyholes
and gouged the ears

and eyes of the world
which wants, we hear,
to send warrants for us
to join all others

on some drill field
of the passions.

But our wars are here—
with the tripping rug,

the acute gods
of solitaire
or the seated one
across from us.

Our accomplishments
are of chairs.
The blankets about our knees
are flecked with snow

that never melts,
that is not real snow.
Our heroes are the mailman
or paperboy—those

who fight the sidewalks
in all weathers.
Our only real enemy
is the prowler, uninvited,

who wants to wound
our chairs or break
the seals on our roofs
and let the wilting sunlight in.

PART IV

Today is Monday

As if unsure of its date,
the day begins slowly—
like an old pump
being primed: I remember

that dry cough before
water came, tasting faintly
of obscure ores, so cold
it buried an ache

behind your forehead.
And today, chimes labor
in the winter air
as I make my way into the world,

exploring a day that feels
so much like the others—balanced
on the lip of the week. My feet
look for the stairs

and the ritual of razor
and lather, the taste
of toothpaste on my tongue.
But there is something I try

to remember: a question
asked in a dream,
a face lost in deep caverns
where we swam all night long,

brushed by fish with soft fins.
I think of another country
with a name like Venezuela,
but not Venezuela, where waterfalls

never hold still for the tourist's
camera, where we will eat
food with a name like avocado.
I glimpse this while I shave—

behind the mirror, cramped among
the milling reflections
it has saved. Go slow, I think,
the mirror is too deep; your world

goes the other way, righthanded.
I know I will put yesterday's coins
back in my pockets—shields to stop bullets—
but I guide the razor carefully today.

Late October

The given moment
has stopped in my
watch. Light gropes
through clouds
toward the sundial
on the mortuary lawn.
Without light, it
has stopped too.

Down the next street
an exile looks
for the home he
lost, now painted
over or torn from
the telephone book.
All that is left,
a basement looking
bombed out, lies open,
drowning in the rain.

Tomorrow the mush-
room experts will be
out, surgeon fingers
picking warts
from the grass.
Now toadstools tense
before thrusting
through the lawns,
shoulders hunched,
disguised as mush-
rooms. I shrug too,
uneasy in my disguise,
the fat burgher,
the lover of life.

The Spare Room

You lie awake. The attic
begins its nightly act.
Moths stir, going through
old pockets; rafters strain
still thinking themselves
the fine bones in wings,
the shingles feathers.

It is taking you to sleep,
to the place of old pictures
and clothes you have
outgrown. In the dark
the clock face shines.
You angle backward into
time. This is the room

of childhood where your
sleeping body counted bruises
all night long as warm
shadows moved above you,
comfort in their hands,
and walked into the premises
of your dream. They are gone now.

The only place you meet them
is in your sleep. You know
there has been some mistake;
they are out there still, beyond
the edges of your sleep, tiptoeing,
holding the night together until
morning comes. And then it comes.

Gilbert & Market

Today the sun's blades slide
through the worn bamboo blind
and in the store below
people are playing bingo
on the cash register
while I try to haunt my mind
with names like Dachau,
Buchenwald or Hiroshima.

But how do you speak
of such things in any terms today
in a room where the sun
distracts, edited into arrows
by the slats of the blind?
What words will carry terror
in a place where the typewriter
weighs heavy with demands

like a medal made of a millstone?
where there are books, gaunt
and worn, that refuse to spit
their knowledge even though
you break their bindings?
How are such specters of the private
made public ghosts? Downstairs
people are buying out the store

and here books of words lie
dormant and thoughts corrode
the bland surfaces of paper. Below
they are filling a vacancy
their distended cupboards have
never known, assuring themselves

that if all else fails at least
they won't feel the mice

of hunger at their bellies.
Who can tell them that hunger
lives best in the ripe heart
of abundance? They thrive
on this art of taking.
They have finally lost their
childhoods and become adults
with accounts of their own

to overdraw; they have
their own lives like new toys
that demand destruction.
Meanwhile, they buy meat.
There are enough horrors
to blunt any pen today—
people whirr like flies
in rooms below, workmen

with pneumatic drills repair
the street by digging huge
chunks from your consciousness.
What to say? Keep at it, men,
and then go home and wallow
in your canned goods? The strongest
attention is broken by their drills,
the weakest shattered by the sun.

The century is like a large
animal breathing the odors
of its disease above the town.
How does the mind deal with
this malignant time, these

years that grow fat on death
and slake their thirst for chaos
every decade? Casualties

have been piled so high
the senses will not register
death in numbers. Which
among our rusting instruments
will gauge this time
on such a day when typewriters
chew at our fingers
and women in shorts walk

through the spattered sunlight
showing thighs which promise
that though the world may fall
they may spread and let us
conquer it again? The heavy
industry of hate burns factory
lights all night. Deceit
is nurtured in all the gardens

of diplomacy. And the people
in the store below are starving,
laughing and starving. And the women
on the street wear the thick
ankles of embarrassment;
acne scars the surfaces
of their romance packaged
in magazines about their favorite

movie star who sleeps with them
in dreams. Something tears
at the maps we live on;
something mutters in the spaces

between our walls. Like all towns
this town sports its bullseye
and is mounted on someone's chart
like an insect pierced by a pin.

We do not come to terms.
History is ravenous about us.
The sun is burning to a cinder
outside the blinds. Intricate
pressures are building up
below the earth's fetid rind
and we are forced to follow
this century's crippled path.

Getting Through the Day

We begin with false starts:
light stutters, the stairs
complain, the necktie
unravels and I hide
its stain in the knot.
Goodbye at the door—
a kiss slides away—
and I steer the old car

into its ruts. False starts
all day: prefatory nods,
introductory smiles. The actors
perform. Hello. Hello. Hello
to the cold wind. I hear
the lies in a tone of voice.
Speaking, the gears slip,
membranes break, I follow

illness back to a wish.
Meaning No we nod Yes,
signing confessions with our
faces. The brackets of work
fall away, a paragraph
concludes. Indifferent to
the outcome of this game
until the end, we find

the loser was our favorite;
five o'clock, the score
paralyzed into history
by the final gun. Goodbye.
We hear those campers,
cancer cells, gather in the twilight.
On the way home the wheels
pound loss. I remember the lies.

The Window

Outside, I walk across the street—
old, cradling a six-pack with arms of chalk
as bells in towers chip pieces from the night.

I stroll along the staggering sidewalk
and from here, this dated day, this window,
the broken rudder of my mind
drifts among the noises of the street
that is the debris of another, future evening.

The bells chip and pick. I walk on.
My belt strains at the round insistence
of my stomach. My feet,
wearing their awards of broken arches,
recoil from stubborn concrete.
Lamplight bathes my bald head;
shadows fall, sifting in the wrinkles
gathered near my eyes.

I sit. The window accepts the rumors
of the wind. Blind trucks run the roads,
their knuckles cracking as gears shift,
carrying cargoes of wealth to someone else.

Outside, I walk on,
numb flightless bird settled in age,
still shuffling toward the future's nets—
now an empty jar, a burnt-out match.
The soot of years settles relentlessly
as I walk toward some dim bulb
remembering myself now—
how I sat plunging thoughts of a future
into the sponge heart of the street.

At the window I hear a desolate phone
ring across lawns of charcoal;
a screen door opens
giving its harsh reply,
a parrot's feeble squawk,
and the old man's memory climbs the stairs
looking for the vacant place
left for him at my table.

The Adventurer

1.

I think of you, burned black
　　by that tropic sun
　　you carry like a kite
　　above your knapsack,

Your mind's edge rubbed sharp
　　by the chips of stone
　　that are your eyes,
　　while I plow deeper

Every year waiting for that day
　　when fields lie completely
　　fallow and I've taken root
　　so deeply that even envy

Will run thin, watered down
　　with some commonplace sap
　　of this countryside.
　　While your feet barely indent

The sand that litters scenarios,
　　I sink in mud. My roots
　　are still tendrils, blind
　　as worms and afraid of the dark.

2.

I stay here watching my thoughts
　　of voyages whiten on the banks
　　of the river of mud I navigate;
　　they become the imaginary

Silver dollars I throw across.
    (We become heroes as best we can.)
    But then I think of you
    threading trails through

The jungles of your desire
    and my despair. Something
    withers when I think of this.
    You pay no income tax.

All your papers are really forged
    while mine seem false
    only because the State
    lacks subtlety—my ID card

Identifies someone else,
    an approximation of myself,
    not myself. I am
    the document that is forged.

    3.
Each night you slam
    through my dreams
    on the Orient Express.
    The best I can do

Is to spread my toast extravagantly
    with butter or scandalize
    my stomach with 3.2 beer.
    Each morning I secure

My head with a necktie,
    emblem of the hate that waits
    in the plump hearts of families
    and shows itself at Christmas,

As you swim the heavy oil
        of the Congo or parachute
        behind the lines of my childhood.
        You always go; I always stay,

Remaining a spy without orders
        or purpose. My tunnels
        of escape are always found;
        my compatriots are all informers.

Your actions comment on my life,
        but you smudge your face
        for maneuvers behind the wrong lines.
        Here the war is endless, the enemy obscure.